Little People, **BIG DREAMS**
ELLA FITZGERALD

Written by
Mª Isabel Sánchez Vegara

Illustrated by
Bàrbara Alca

Translated by
Raquel Plitt

Lincoln
Children's Books

Little Ella grew up in Yonkers, New York,
with her mother, stepfather, and sister.
She had a beautiful voice
and loved to sing jazz.

But one day, tragedy struck. Her mother
died suddenly in a car accident.
Ella was heartbroken.

Ella went to live with her aunt, but she didn't like her new life. She started skipping school and got into trouble, so she was sent to a strict school as punishment. She was treated very badly there—so one day, she ran away . . .

Ella made a living by singing and dancing
on the street corners of Harlem.
The street was her first stage!

But one night, she entered a competition to perform on a real stage—at one of the most famous theaters in New York. She was very nervous, but dazzled the crowd with her sweet, tuneful voice. She won first prize!

That night, Ella was so excited she couldn't sleep. She imagined herself singing on an even bigger stage, accompanied by her very own orchestra.

It wasn't long before big band leader Chick Webb offered Ella her first singing job. Together, they traveled all over the country performing in jazz clubs. Ella's career was taking off!

CHICK WEBB

Ella never sang a song the same way twice.
She turned somersaults with her voice and learned
to imitate every instrument in the band.

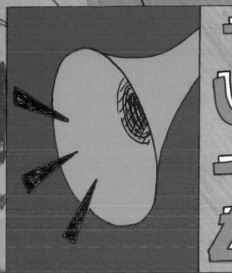

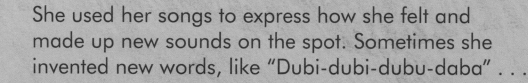

She used her songs to express how she felt and made up new sounds on the spot. Sometimes she invented new words, like "Dubi-dubi-dubu-daba" . . .

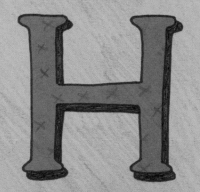

She also sang slow songs as sweet as lullabies. Her velvety voice wrapped around the audience like a blanket.

Eventually, Ella decided it was time
to leave the band and go solo.

All the jazz greats wanted to perform with her. The telephone didn't stop ringing!

Ella tried every musical style, from bop to swing. Her voice growled, swooped, and soared. She mastered show tunes, pop, opera, and blues, taking her music to new places until the day she retired.

And that's how little Ella became the First Lady of Song.
As she always said, "It isn't where you came from;
it's where you're going that counts."

ELLA FITZGERALD

(Born 1917 • Died 1996)

c. 1930

1938

From an early age, Ella Fitzgerald had a passion for dance and
an ear for music. She grew up in New York, around the time the
biggest names in jazz were performing in the city. Young Ella would
take the train to Harlem to see her favorite musicians. But her life
changed forever in 1932, when her mother died in a car accident.
Ella was only 15, and she found it hard to adjust to life without her.
She was sent to a strict school, known as a reform school, but she
was treated badly, so she ran away. This was the time of the Great
Depression in America, when people were struggling to make ends
meet, and Ella had to dance on the streets of Harlem to make
enough money to survive. But one night, at age 17, she entered

c. 1940   1965

the Apollo Theater's amateur talent competition. Ella was planning
to dance, but changed her mind when she saw another dance act
perform. She decided to sing instead. Ella won first prize and was
later spotted by band leader Chick Webb. Together, they had a hit
with a song called "A-Tisket, A-Tasket." Ella went on to have a 50-
year musical career. She recorded over 2,000 songs and worked
with all the jazz greats. She was the first African American woman
to win a Grammy, adding 12 more to her collection throughout her
lifetime. With her sweet, uplifting voice and talent for rhythm, Ella
became known as the "First Lady of Song"—and one of the best
jazz singers of the 20th century.

Want to find out more about **Ella Fitzgerald**?
Read these great books:

Skit-Scat Raggedy Cat: Ella Fitzgerald by Roxane Orgill and Sean Qualls

Ella, Queen of Jazz by Helen Hancocks

Ella Fitzgerald: The Tale of a Vocal Virtuosa by Andrea Davis Pinkney and Brian Pinkney

Brimming with creative inspiration, how-to projects, and useful information to enrich your everyday life, Quarto Knows is a favourite destination for those pursuing their interests and passions. Visit our site and dig deeper with our books into your area of interest: Quarto Creates, Quarto Cooks, Quarto Homes, Quarto Lives, Quarto Drives, Quarto Explores, Quarto Gifts, or Quarto Kids.

Inspiring | Educating | Creating | Entertaining

Text © 2017 Mª Isabel Sánchez Vegara. Illustrations © 2017 Bàrbara Alca
First published in the U.S.A. in 2018 by Lincoln Children's Books, an imprint of The Quarto Group.
400 First Avenue North, Suite 400, Minneapolis, MN 55401, USA.
T (612) 344-8100 F (612) 344-8692 **www.QuartoKnows.com**

First published in Spain in 2017 under the title Pequeña & Grande Ella Fitzgerald
by Alba Editorial, s.l.u., Baixada de Sant Miquel, 1, 08002 Barcelona
www.albaeditorial.es
All rights reserved.
Translation rights arranged by IMC Agència Literària, SL

ISBN 978-1-78603-087-0

The illustrations were created in pencil and ink, then colored digitally
Set in Futura BT
Published by Rachel Williams • Designed by Karissa Santos
Edited by Katy Flint • Production by Kate O'Riordan
Manufactured in Guangdong, China CC in 012018

9 8 7 6 5 4 3 2 1

MIX
Paper from
responsible sources
FSC® C008047

Photographic acknowledgements (pages 28–29, from left to right) 1. Ella Fitzgerald portrait, c.1930 © Everett Collection Inc / Alamy Stock Photo 2. Ella Fitzgerald, 1938 © Getty 3. Ella Fitzgerald Portrait, c. 1940s © Glasshouse Images / Alamy Stock Photo 4. Ella Fitzgerald, US jazz singer, 1965 © Pictorial Press Ltd / Alamy Stock Photo

Also in the *Little People,* **BIG DREAMS** series:

FRIDA KAHLO

ISBN: 978-1-84780-783-0

Meet Frida Kahlo, one of the best artists of the twentieth century.

COCO CHANEL

ISBN: 978-1-84780-784-7

Discover the life of Coco Chanel, the famous fashion designer.

MAYA ANGELOU

ISBN: 978-1-84780-889-9

Read about Maya Angelou —one of the world's most beloved writers.

AMELIA EARHART

ISBN: 978-1-84780-888-2

Learn about Amelia Earhart—the first female to fly solo over the Atlantic.

AGATHA CHRISTIE

ISBN: 978-1-84780-960-5

Meet the queen of the imaginative mystery— Agatha Christie.

MARIE CURIE

ISBN: 978-1-84780-962-9

Be introduced to Marie Curie, the Nobel Prize-winning scientist.

ROSA PARKS

ISBN: 978-1-78603-018-4

Discover the life of Rosa Parks, the first lady of the civil rights movement.

AUDREY HEPBURN

ISBN: 978-1-78603-053-5

Learn about the iconic actress and humanitarian— Audrey Hepburn.

EMMELINE PANKHURST

ISBN: 978-1-78603-020-7

Meet Emmeline Pankhurst, the suffragette who helped women get the vote.

ADA LOVELACE

ISBN: 978-1-78603-076-4

Read all about Ada Lovelace, the first computer programmer.

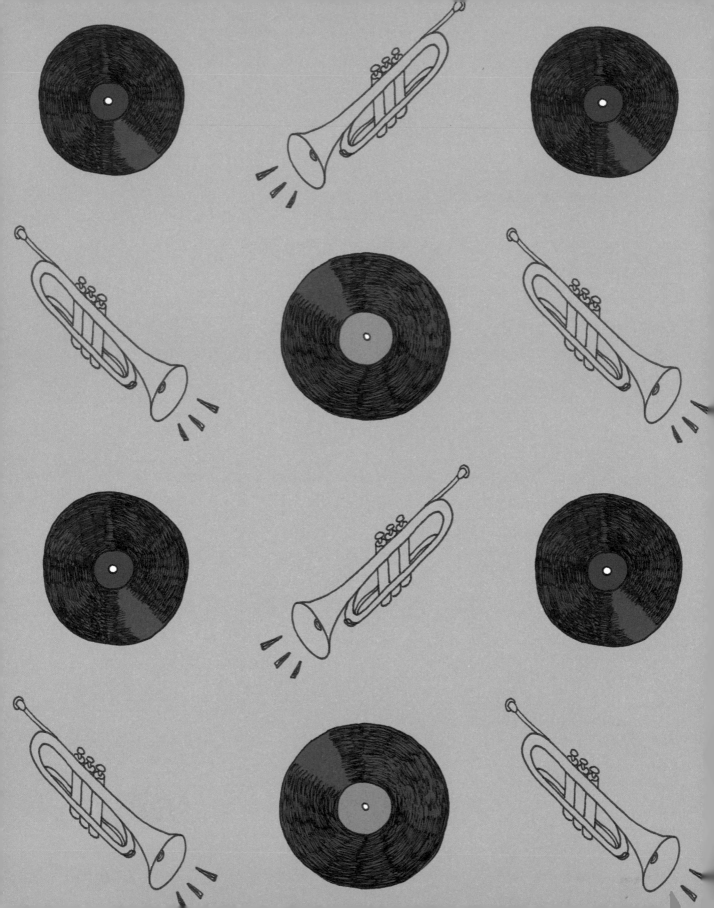